Sun Dogs

Sun Dogs

poems by
Anthony Labriola

Shanti Arts Publishing
Brunswick, Maine

Sun Dogs

Copyright © 2020 Anthony Labriola

All Rights Reserved
No part of this book may be used or reproduced in any manner whatsoever without the written permission of the publisher.

Published by Shanti Arts Publishing
Interior and cover design by Shanti Arts Designs

Shanti Arts LLC
193 Hillside Road
Brunswick, Maine 04011
shantiarts.com

The title of the cover image is *Vädersolstavlan,* which is Swedish for The Sundog Painting. An oil-on-panel painting, it depicts sun dogs, an atmospheric optical phenomenon observed over Stockholm on April 20, 1535. While chiefly noted for being the oldest depiction of Stockholm in color, it is arguably also the oldest Swedish landscape painting and the oldest depiction of sun dogs. The original painting, attributed to Urban målare (Urban [the] Painter), is lost, and virtually nothing is known about it. However, this copy from 1636 by Jacob Heinrich Elbfas is held in Storkyrkan (Stockholm Cathedral). It was previously covered by layers of brownish varnish, and the image was hardly discernible until it was carefully restored in 1998–99.
<https://en.wikipedia.org/wiki/V%C3%A4dersolstavlan>

Printed in the United States of America

ISBN: 978-1-951651-52-7 (softcover)
ISBN: 978-1-951651-53-4 (hardcover)

Library of Congress Control Number: 2020945818

*To my beloved mother and father and my
wonderful brothers and sisters—
all of whom are members of my family planetarium.*

*To my wife, Louisa Josephine, and our awesome star-children,
including our daughter-in-law and son-in-law.*

To our incredible grandchildren—journeying to a new world.

*To all my friends—
even those on the lost planets of the past.*

Contents

Acknowledgments	*11*

Prologue
Galaxy	17

Planetarium
Sun Dogs	21
Alien Warnings	22
Carrying the Sorrow of the Big Bang	23
The Family Planetarium	24
The Devisers	25
Mythic Thinking	26
In the Event of Death Rays	27
Inner Space	28
Tracking Stars	29
The Blessed Virgin Mary In a Space Suit	30
This Wonder	31
Under the Influence of Venus	32
River Capture	33
Snow-flowers	34
Catching a Bird	35
Reading the Room	36
Drawing a Spacecraft	37
When Apollo 11 Landed	38
Leaving August	39
No Closure	40
Qwerty Uiop	41
Storms In Space	42

Star Wheel 43
Saving the Planetarium 44
Basket of Stars 45

Jealous Planet

Sun Spots 49
How Easy Everything Is
   When You Can't See It 50
Night with Telescope 51
Reading the Earth 52
In the Direction of Her Body 53
First Love 54
Illustrated Kiss 55
Gaze 56
The Blessings of Madness 57
Jumper 58
Jealous Planet 59
Assumption 60
Wedding in the Woods 61
In the Embrace of Seventeenth-
   Century Architecture 62
Wayward Moon 63
Ask the Words 64
Intimacy 65
Leaving the Floating Island 66
Piercing Notes 67
Exploding Flower 68
Blood Stars 69
Substitutions 70
Capturing the Artist 71
Losers Weepers 72
Mapping the Hidden City 73
Street Busker 74

Between My Toes	75
Begging at My Own Door	76

Cosmic Therapies

Therapy of the Final Approach	81
Cosmic Therapy	82
Therapy of the Last Ditch	83
Therapy of Faint Praise	84
Therapy of Empty Rooms	85
Therapy of the Visible World	86
Therapy of the Trickster Sun	87
Therapy of a Mountain Session	88
Therapy of Being in the World	89
Therapy of Living in a Terrarium	90
Therapy of Losing Your Mother Tongue	92
Therapy of Absence	93
Therapy of Being Hurt into Love	94
Therapy of Losing You	95
Therapy of High-Climbing	96
Therapy of Sorrow	97
Therapy of Coming and Going	98
Therapy of Silent Films	99
Therapy of the Echo	102
Therapy of Scavenging	103
Therapy of Reading the Woods	104
Therapy of Stargazing	105

Epilogue

Until Every Sky Repairs Its Stars	111

About the Author	*113*

Acknowledgments

"Assumption" appeared in *The Canadian Forum* as "Untitled."

"Therapy of Silent Films" appeared in *Prisminternational* as "Silent Films."

"Basket of Stars," "High-Climbing," and "Losers Weepers" appeared in *Vallum Magazine*.

My gratitude goes to Christine Cote for her kindness, generosity, and compassion.

Sun dogs appear as bright spots to the left and right of the sun. In winter, sun dogs appear on the inner halo. When the sun is high, sun dogs show up outside the halo. Though rare, moon dogs come out at night.

Prologue

Galaxy

I almost escaped the riddling road that forked
into the highway's crossroad where my journey met
a doomed chariot and rider. I trailed dark blood
into the fabled woods and fell asleep

with no one to wake me from this ageless epic
that sprang fully grown out of my forehead, and groaning
grew into the image and likeness of the sun-
headed east. Prophecy pierced my anklebones;

a riddle thrashed my skull. The black-robed west splattered
my bowels on stone. Northern witches predicted
my father's murder. The spiteful southern gate

led to the core. To map the hero's body,
I found the victim's pattern in entrails and organs—
odyssey of the body's inner galaxy.

one

Planetarium

Sun Dogs

When I tracked the turning sky with blaze-bright
haloes—solar and lunar—I was running
with the sun dogs, baying with the moon dogs.
I was mocked by other tricks of light. My star

atlas was a night-sky with or without
the blue-eyed lens of a telescope. Now you see it,
now you don't—the bright smirk of the mock sun
and the curled lip of the moon. The sky turned around

and I ran from the dogs, hid myself from sightings
of lesser lights. Recorded other tricks and buried
my tracks. But the hounds pursued me in blind-sight.

In a galaxy of naked eyes, my optic nerves,
in point-and-shoot, shot the sun and moon,
revealed the planets to unveil the all-seeing sky.

Alien Warnings

> *The human race shouldn't have all its eggs in one basket, or on one planet. Let's hope we can avoid dropping the basket until we have spread the load.*
> —Stephen Hawking

Alien warnings murmured: *Abandon Earth*

before being swallowed by the Sun. Hawking,
in a talking wheelchair, spoke of eggs in one
basket; or on one planet, of spreading the load.

In an ark of perpetual night, I reached
the launch site; commenced the full-throated
countdown. On bending light, I surrendered to life

elsewhere; moved on to the nearest star.
But I carried birds in my pockets, nesting,
chirruping; twigs and bits of string, traces of

the place, alluvial soil and blue eggs
cupped in my hands; gestures of saving the planet
from and for myself. I tried not to drop

my one load: a basketful of old earth.

Carrying the Sorrow of the Big Bang

I tried to escape the fabled world. Flung to
the farthest reaches, I carried the sorrow
of the Big Bang in my guts. Attached to the route,
my body endured the image and likeness

of time and space. The last days surged, like lost waves,
towards the last moment. Time zones switched to
what I thought I was after—the origin of death.

But nothing could keep me from jumping. In red
auroras, no-fly zones sustained the fatal sky.
I prevailed. Black feathers fell, floated and covered

the doomed stars. Light-bearing torrents of red-
to-violet waves determined twenty-three times
the Sun-Earth distance. Inscribed on my eyelids,
constellations banged off their new stars and planets.

The Family Planetarium

> *Love, that is all the earth to lovers—*
> *love, that mocks time and space,*
> *Love, that is day and night—love, that*
> *is sun and moon and stars,*
> *Love, that is crimson, sumptuous, sick with perfume,*
> *No other words but words of love, no other thought but love.*
> —Walt Whitman, "The Mystic Trumpeter,"
> *Leaves of Grass*

The family as a planetarium:
my father and mother as sun and moon—

the rest as planets in their gravitational
pull. In the family planetary system,

we are phantom planets and our world is a jealous
place in the sphere of floating lives that attract

and repel each other—living and dead.
I touched the cold beauty of celestial

body parts, but rebelled against my own
orbit. Under the threat of ticking stars,

to the soundtrack of Holst, I mapped my dying
stars. In a spray of tongued notes, the mystic

trumpeter blew a new heaven and earth,
but spat me out, like spit from his spit valve.

The Devisers

Under the cardinal, fixed and mutable
signs of the zodiac, I crawled on hands
and knees to ask devisers of inter-
planetary legends, and ones that can't
be devised, what they had to say about
my search, but they merely hummed a tune
from the music of the spheres. I glossed
fairy tales, myths, sagas and stories,
but they wouldn't break their vows or give up
their dead. So I asked the *words* what to say.
Let your quest find its sudden reversal,
they said. *Let it happen as if by itself.*
Kill the first person in favor of the third.
My mother sided with the moon and stars.

But my father took the sun's part with a keen
eye on Saturn. The lunar opposed
the solar. In disputes about the past,
I played peekaboo with dwarf planets
and near planets. Despite my mother's
precautions, my father, like Saturn, sat
eating his sons, fearing revolt only
to vomit us up again, at my mother's
shrill insistence. On that incandescent
day, when he ate and spat me out,
I was flung into the night sky to hatch
rebellions. And despite paternal laws,
and the moans of the groaning ground, I gathered
a brother or two to bring our sun down.

Mythic Thinking

I asked wordsmiths on this and other planets
about the source of my rebellion. *You don't
envy the sun*, they intoned, *as reported in
your chronicles, but Saturn is jealous of you.*

*He trembles at how many rebels he has
to roast and eat.* Wasn't that what my father
was afraid of, riding in his royal
chariot to the oracle to know his fate?

I struck him down where three roads met and walked
away with pierced feet. In the throes of mythic thought,
I riddled down the road on two legs that noon,

only to twist and tap with a stick in the blind-
folded night. Like my father before me, I lived
in a myth devised before we were born.

In the Event of Death Rays

For my father, words were two-faced liars
that kept their heads down in the event of death rays.
Every mouth opened and closed with lies.

Every liar has mud in his mouth, he said,
and every mouth is a dirty liar.
And with his skeleton finger on the trigger,

my father fired his homemade weapon,
and shattered the spine of my shooting star.
His mouth did all the killing; words did the rest.

In a blaze of talk, as if it speaking truth, he said:
Get out of your head and into your senses.
But you can't escape your inscape, can you?

So tell it as if from the Book of Job, saying,
'They're all dead. I alone escaped to tell it.'

Inner Space

Threading through my veins visits from inner
space, exploding suns of jealousy and rage,
galaxies of panic and love, an alien

fix of supernovas, lungs of forgotten
prayers, and cannibalized words of warring
worlds. Absent without leave, the leave-taking,

longed for in this odyssey, got me out
of my head and my eyes blasted off
with inward signs of blind-sight. I trusted

the blindfold. In a year of coming through,
I went on and in. Ventured outside
the planetarium. Told how and why

I left home. Moved on the first wave of the first
cause, and told how the place smelled of tears.

Tracking Stars

The footbridge, once leading to the schoolyard,

is gone. And so is the frame house on Nassau
Street. There, I played my Atomic Age games.
In the event of a death cloud, not *stop*,

drop and roll, but *duck and cover*, from the
observation tower in my bedroom,
I read torn maps of the ticklish universe.

Made bombs and threw my body on them
in a loving embrace. But the tracking
of stars never ends. I go round and round

in a tiny solar system of love
and jealousy. Now, deadlights argue for the past.
I'm arguing with the dead, whispering then shouting

that once, up in my bedroom, I tracked the stars.

The Blessed Virgin Mary
In a Space Suit

I slipped through thin ice into rapid, reversing waters.
When fast currents captured, pulled and pushed
my shocked, wet body, I bobbed up and down,
like a seal pup in an ice-capped aquarium.

I squirmed beneath silver-blue ice. But fast
and faster, my brother thrust a hand in
to pluck me out, sleek as a creek otter.
Hoisted me up onto his padded shoulders

and carried me home, a wet, crying load.
Up to our bedroom, the back way, my skin
trembled gooseflesh. I tried to keep from shivering.

Just then, my mamma appeared in the doorway,
blue rays shooting from her long fingernails,
the Blessed Virgin Mary in a space suit.

This Wonder

It was a gift that had a name – this wonder

that I'd blundered into. A kind of
name-poem with my name in it, as if Vincent
Van Gogh wrote me postcards in cadmium yellow

and cobalt blue and saw me skin my knees
in a field of lifting blackbirds. The Sunday
morning gift of finding loose change outside

the Cadillac Hotel, and the wonder of falling
off my cousin's bike, sitting on the handlebars
between his two hands. Then my tangled foot

got mangled in the spokes, and we rode home
on a wobbly wheel and bent fork. But despite the blood
on our jeans, coins jiggled in our pockets—

with us giggling in the language of being thirteen.

Under the Influence of Venus

It was good to have Bucky on my left,
all buckteeth and cigarette glued to your rotting
lower lip. It was better to have Dexter
on my right, freckled, and walking off-kilter
from a swift kick to the balls. But best was
putting arms around our shoulders, calling,
Army, Army. Bucky looked like a Martian.

And Dexter wore his crew cut like a space helmet.
Feet turned inward, he could hardly walk from the pain
in his groin. Myles had kicked him, gripped and
　milked him
from behind. In a fight over Cindy,
a Grade 8 Venusian, he was impervious to
the influence of Venus. And on the schoolyard,
he didn't know what real love was, or how it hurt.

River Capture

In the terrain of letting go of boys
pissing in the creek, I searched for sticks
for my longbow, and plucked the bowstring,
for the sake of the twang. I gathered stones

for my slingshot. Electric shocks shot
and surged from fingertips to funny bone.
No Huck Finn or Big Jim on a fast raft,
I read rapids backwards and shivered in

river capture. But on the bank, I jumped
off a red maple and plummeted to the ground
in the sudden realization of how
gravity can snap an arm in two, and does.

The terrain won't let go of the primitive brain.
It captures a boy's dreams and takes no prisoners.

SNOW-FLOWERS

Snowflakes on my papa's tongue, he spits them
out. Piles into a half-ton pickup
truck. *Roofing* rages across it in

red. A witch's pot is hitched to the back
on tar-spattered, white-walled wheels. Wintering on
a snowbound highway, my papa lifts off,

a winter bird ascending, and crash-lands
in a ditch. Back home, we're praying for
his safe return. The corollas of our

candles burn down their stems. Then better
than any birthday, he steps in, wearing
snow-flowers plucked from the side of the highway—

winter's garden of tiny miracles—
flowering snowflakes of our answered prayers.

Catching a Bird

An old running shoe will do as home plate.
Long laces dangle and stretch out like grass
snakes. A ruby-throated hummingbird
hovers in the outfield. A pitch, and my bat

goes flying against a neighbor's garage.
Still, it's a home run—tiny victory,
like balancing a Louisville Slugger
on the tip of my nose—I can still do that trick.

But my mamma is pegging wet washing
on the clothesline. Rounding third, I dart for home,
holler, *Don't catch it. Don't catch the ball, Ma.*

Yet in the fate of backyard ballgames, and pop flies,
she makes a perfect catch, shouting, *Caught it, caught it*—
as if catching a bird with a bare, wet hand.

Reading the Room

My cracked lens glimpses a paint-by-number
portrait on the living room wall. And in
the front hall, it stares at a print of Dante
observing Beatrice, crossing a bridge.

Then reads the room by an evening star.
Our tidy house is made even tidier
by Mamma as she prays to Vesta,
Roman goddess of the hearth. She stares out

the kitchen window through lace curtains—
the ones she brought with her in a steamer trunk
on April 15, 1953.

Upstairs, my older brother dips his brush
into a jar of cosmic colors, and, slantwise,
on the windowpane, slashes a shooting star.

Drawing a Spacecraft

I'm on a secret mission in my bedroom,
1957, filled with envy.
From his own designs, my older brother
is building a flying saucer in the attic—a young
da Vinci drawing a spacecraft, locking it and loading
it in an irreversible countdown sequence,
if only he can find a way to get it out of there.

Now, in the basement, I'm working on shooting it
down from the stars. My weapon is still top secret,
under wraps. In my jealousy, I'm up
for sabotage and humiliation.
I'm keeping a close watch on the launch
to get the plans for the project, or failing that,
to commandeer the rocket that envies its flight.

When Apollo 11 Landed

While other kids read the blood-red
testament of war, I rode my red bike—
streamers screaming from high-riding handlebars.
On the spokes, a baseball card, clipped by a clothespin,
picked a plucky tune. The white-walled tires
ballooned my plush seat up off the gravel road.
When Apollo 11 landed, I was playing
ball in the flats. And when a lone gunman
loaded his Italian bolt-action rifle
with the Hollywood scope and took aim
in Dallas at a black limousine, I unclipped
the baseball card and flicked it towards Rainbow
Confectionery for an ice cream cone—one scoop
for every sticky lick of being young.

LEAVING AUGUST

I'm kicking over summer's traces,
1966. Don't want to go back
to school that September, leaving August
for Saturday Night Confession at Holy Cross—

hoping to get Father Burial,
instead of Father Coffin. I'm called to sin
with cigarettes and skin mags and cough up
coins at the variety store close to the church.

But the only choice that night is Father C.,
yelling in the box: *You did what? What the hell for?*
An Act of Contrition, a Glory Be,

two Our Fathers, and one Hail Mary—he doesn't
know how sorry I am. Communion wine on his breath—
Go and sin no more, he says. And I mouth: *Amen.*

No Closure

Remember the way the confession ends,

my mother said. But I told her a tall tale
to get back what I'd lost—to finish telling it
once and for all. That we appear to each other

as lesser lights—as dim reflectors of love;
optical illusions that dance before the light.
But nothing in childhood had prepared me

for this: the dream-within-the-dream motif
of Edgar Allen Poe—or the dream that dies
with the dreamer—as if closure is what we call

the end. No closure when falling asleep—
no forgiveness in the persistence of dreams,
when waking dispenses with the therapy

of stargazing and the saga of a dying sun.

Qwerty Uiop

Polychrome rock paintings on the cave walls
of Altamira depict me sitting
in profile in front of a borrowed
typewriter. The Underwood, descendant
of the Gatling gun, types what comes out,
unasked for, improvised, and unanswered
in those clicking, clacking days. Keys skip,

and I strike the missing letters of a lost
alphabet. Spools of black and red shuttle
to and fro. I claw the keys, as if typing
words on a cave wall. Or—*polychrome cave*
paintings on the walls of Altamira
represent me seated in profile
clawing the keys of a borrowed typewriter.

Storms In Space

From the second-storey observatory,
I charted the gathering storm. The weather's

warriors threw down their lightning shields,
emblazoned with storms in space. In the sway

of rebellious wind, leaves rioted on Nassau Street,
and golden hordes rode in with war drums and red

banners. My little sisters, soaked to the skin,
were running home from school. They almost beat

the thunderstorm to the veranda, as the tail
end lashed the trees in the front yard.

I stepped back from the dark window, lit up
by forked lightning, just as another invader

set out from the heartland of hurricanes in space
to count the storm's victims and nature's dead.

STAR WHEEL

Stars in the January sky wheel above
our house. At the *séance*, we hold hands and wait
for the apparition; our papa's ghost.
Is that moonlight? I ask. *Or fatal starlight?*
But what do I know about quarter turns
of the star wheel, or the sheeted dead? All
that's required is holding hands with the dead.
Afraid of the bony fingers of his hand,
I'm disinclined to do this and claw my way
through the bodiless room, its vaulted ceiling
painted with lost stars. When I leave the *séance*,
I enter the night as full of pulsars
as the planetarium will allow.
Papa's ghost is the bringer of old age.

Saving the Planetarium

That's how it is on this bitch of an earth.
—Samuel Beckett

Sometimes, it's too much to be on the earth,
and sometimes not enough. It was foretold
that I'd walk on the creek, like a Jesus Lizard
walking on water, when I'm not afraid.

And when I am, I cast my net skyward.
But the day is meant for cleaning the house,
or going for a walk in the symbolic woods.
I pick up trash from the side of the highway

to protect the landfill I used to call *the dump*.
Paper, tires, hubcaps, bottles, plastic bags—
the lifelessness that will outlive me;
the unsaved detritus of living here.

But in a new parable, I'm making gestures
of saving the planet from its broken heart.

Basket of Stars

The meaning of silence or rain—the silence

against which one can hear the cries of a dying
star, or a star child—then we pull back
the hoods of our black sweatshirts, like novices

seeking sunlight on the seven-storey mountain.
We'll hear a voice warning us as we move away,
but we'll already have made our decision.

Towards a new beginning at the end,
both better and worse than before, we'll collide
with one of our possible futures, or all

of them at once. As if it were totally
impossible, we'll leave the Earth without breaking
all the eggs in the basket of what is

about to be: a basket full of stars.

two

Jealous Planet

Sun Spots

While I was in the world, I tried to bring light.
Through time-zones, I arrived at new destinations.
Often, the longing for the past was so present
that I traveled back. But today and tomorrow
rescued me from yesterday. Despite departures
and arrivals, the time-traveler and the sky-watcher
sometimes knew each other without knowing it.

In an eclipse of the moon, ramparts, ridges
and soaring cliffs rose up along the coast—and standing
stones reached up like mutilated fingers.
In a manned space flight, my wings were made
out of feathers and wax. I collided
with fatal light but my father escaped
the fall with sunspots on his blinded eyes.

How Easy Everything Is When You Can't See It

I'm looking for birds I can't name – not those
I can: robins, sparrows, blue jays, cardinals,
red-winged blackbirds, or even yellow warblers –
always cropping up in my field notes.

I'm searching for the ones you can't see
in the slaughter of birds. But are they enough
when the list is so simple? Why name them
if they'll show up here, anyway, as more

than images of birds—species of
a new earth I'm looking for—natural
laws, suspended, speeded-up, or slowed-down.

It's expected that you can name what you see.
But blinded by the flight of a silver dove,
who names nature when you can't see it?

Night with Telescope

I yearn to see you. My homemade telescope,
at the wrong end, is an unblinking eye,

dead set against the latest theory
about Roswell. Conspiratorial sightings

are familiar in ways I can't deny.
I search out the night sky for ghost lights

from your window and wait for an alien
abduction, but refracted light tilts the axis

of my looking glass eyes. At night, my telescope
is searching for the diamond planet millions

of light years away. Our sun is a jeweler's lens.
But what can I identify that is not you?

Beyond the whirling violations of what I see,
landing lights guide me to the sight of you.

Reading the Earth

The student nurse sits on the fountain's stone lip.
Rests elbows on her knees. Hands on chin.
From time to time, she looks at the statue—
a likeness of herself at 12 or 13—
carved from a single piece of white stone.
Shades hide her eyes. Long hair is crowned with a cap.
Her white uniform rides high on her thighs.

She lies down, sunbathing. Hands rest on hips,
palms downward, knees, slightly bent.
She soaks up the bright light falling on polished stone.
The spray cools her skin. She stirs the water with her hand.
Then looks over at me. I look down.
She heads towards me; slows down; veers left,
appearing almost still, and not completely alone.

In the Direction of Her Body

Moving in the direction of her body,
I veer off course—an ice ball suspended
in mid-air. Faint, falling footsteps are transposed

in her midnight room and hardly make a sucking
noise in bare feet on the hardwood floor. The first
false step I miss on purpose—the exact

moment of the new direction, the altered
sequence. Now, she moves towards me, changing course
towards jealousy, the wordless poetry

of tangled roots that sink down into your groin.
Outside, it's raining acid. Her street burns
in global heat—the sun splits in two.

In the sway of finding her there, I keep
moving in the direction of her body.

First Love

I enter her atmosphere: fragment
of the first place, fragrance of the first smell—
acrid, humid on her skin. She redefines
the commonplace: such as water, day, blue,

wintering. In her one body, loyalties
are divided among lips, hair, feet and breasts—
first love with no basis of comparison.
I'm caught between her and now. What's obvious

in her can't be known or spoken without cost.
Hidden from me, her eyes deflect light,
like a flock of birds landing on water.

Her lips dissect the darkness of first love.
Her kindness is controlling. There's blood on my mouth,
teeth marks on her skin. I re-enter her atmosphere.

Illustrated Kiss

Lifting eyelids and slightly parted lips—

the illustrated kiss is found in
instruction manuals—topographies
that name every part of her. Kept in

forbidden libraries, astrology books
are devoted to plucking out my eyes.
Bookshops are filled with the arcane and broken

eloquence of her breathing. In secret
passages, she unlocks secret passageways—
corridors that lead to her mouth, her native

tongue. The quality of her fingerprints
scars this sheet of paper. Kiss after kiss
separates me from her for too long—and what

happens when I ask her mouth what to say.

Gaze

Her father's gaze was darker than the inner moons
of Uranus. I was walking her home,

and he was back from the shift at the factory—
long leather coat, black lunch pail and black moustache—

and the way he'd escaped from his homeland
by blowing up a bridge. Legend was:

that he'd whittled a bike from a block of wood,
then somehow crossed the ocean. His home was

his promised land. He ended up on the dead end
avenue and the bungalow he built by the tracks.

And walked home that cold December day to stare
at me standing with his daughter. Yet I never

felt the cold except in his gaze, colder
than any ice-ball in the darkness of deep space.

The Blessings of Madness

I'm crazy, but it's better than being sane.
I'm better under the influence of the moon;
lunatic. I'm at my best when I'm frantic;
out of my head. I vault off the fridge;
backflip off the veranda. With the madness
of the flying Wallendas, I carry a girl
on my shoulders, put her on a pedestal
only to throw knives at her later. Then balance
on wires above your sane houses. I'm placid
on the outside, but seething on the inside.
The blessings of madness sharpen my hearing
to the mad whisperings of far-away lives.
I confuse you when I'm certifiable, unblessed—
shock you when you mistake love for madness.

Jumper

Sunday night trains were canceled in both directions.

Stranded passengers scrambled for cell phones.
Their rides were stuck waiting at the train station,
where cabbies dealt with their sudden good fortune.

But in the eastbound commuter train's last
compartment, passengers delivered what little
news they had of the jumper. A kid said

he saw a man dressed like a bird falling
from the sky. The mythmaker's story was dismissed.
In accidental moonlight, buses picked up

the pissed-off commuters, late in getting back.
The mess on the tracks wasn't leaving
anything to chance. When he jumped in front

of the Go train, he was just going home.

Jealous Planet

Breathless voyage in seeing you
dancing with another boy in the gym.
Or kissing your first crush in the high school play,
then sitting in a teacher's car
parked away from the school.
Or driving home from the northern church
with a guy shaped like a knife.
When you walked in the woods with a liquored-up kid,
I was under the bridge and saw you there.
The way jealousy peels off the skin
and bites off a finger or two,
then pulls back the fingernails
and sinks its teeth into raw parts: nose, ears, eyes,
cheekbones, chin that I cut off and eat.

My mouth feeds on a jealous mouth
that eats itself—jealous of my own jealousy.
Jealous of you—
in your communion dress;
in the station wagon with your brothers and sisters;
carried in, sleeping, by your cousin, and kissed;
wearing cat glasses
to watch the Beatles on Ed Sullivan;
or holding a crippled child.
You, in the dorm, playing folk songs with the nuns,
or cycling to the lake to sleep under the stars,
or dancing with a cricket in the cellar.
On a jealous planet,
jealous eyes never look away.

Assumption

There is a picture of our meeting
mid-winter, 1972,
where we are seated on the ruined walls
of a stone bridge. My head is lowered

serious, contemplative in our union.
I'm brushing aside the light snow.
She waits in the quiet assumption
of beauty beneath dark furs. While she

stares into the viewer's important eyes,
I moved my hand across her breasts,
and she happened to close her eyes

in pleasure or pain. The camera
caught this unfortunate move. I believe
you'll discern her loneliness in that photograph.

Wedding in the Woods

Farther away, milkweed melts in green and white.

Black grass pushes filaments out of ash and soot.
Scorched earth from a grass fire with trees still standing.
Brothers and sisters are hidden in the burnt leaves.

You replace a fallen nest on a treetop,
unwilling to climb down for days.
But at the wedding in the woods, your bride

unveils herself. By a mound shaped like an altar,
she unravels your teenage song of songs.
The creek turns moonlight into troubled waters.

Your words are your only guests. Those on the point
of entering are bears and a little girl
from a fairy tale. But, after the wedding,

you escape to your fabled honeymoon.

In the Embrace of Seventeenth-Century Architecture

At first sight, Quebec City cradles us
in morning light, or on a boat cruise at night,
where harbor lights waggle and flash the gull-
thronged boardwalk. In an eastern morning,

we take a carriage ride. The horse's tail
swishes and lashes our knees. We buy street art,
letting the artist pick sketches for fresh-faced
lovers. He says we look like married children.

Lying in a sleepless bed, tangled in
a mandrake root, I'm reading Gaston Miron's
verses, still inside you. Until we honeymoon

in the Laurentian Mountains, the older part
of Quebec City will hold us in the embrace
of seventeenth-century architecture.

Wayward Moon

I took a few steps towards you in moonlight
that sculled along the creek. You lifted up
to me—a long-legged fly winging
above the water. We climbed up the bank,

entangled in roots. I bent down and wrote
your name with a fingernail in red soil.
The night banished nightingales from the healing trees.
I told how I had unearthed signs of intelligent

life and escaped. How, made of the same dust,
I had returned to Earth, saying: *We're not alone.
We just die that way.* A wayward moon cast its rough,

watery eye on us, sitting with bare feet
dangling over the jagged edge—only to end
in the smallest part of letting each other go.

Ask the Words

Sell all the words you own.
    Leave everything behind

and go back to when you were
    their first guest.

Kneel in prayer and listen
    to their breathing.

Hear what comes out
    when we ask the words what to say

with the only questions
    worth asking of them:

How naked shall I be for you?
    How holy to set you free?

How free to be holy?
    How much like you to be naked?

Intimacy

Comparing sounds, you mentioned a cricket
in the field beyond the house—how comforting
the thrum of trains is on the tracks at night,
recollecting the groove of childhood.

I allowed for the chirring noise you make at
the back of your throat, in and out of sleep,
when you turn away from me in bed.
At the opening of a sunflower

outside our window, the chirping of birds
was always enough for you. I needed proof.
But when our dog barked at squirrels, while we were
sitting in the backyard, I talked about

the intimacy of nature, while you compared
silence to the nature of intimacy.

Leaving the Floating Island

A fountain pen fell from my fingertips,
slipped and sank down—a tiny shipwreck
on the seafloor—for fish to wonder at.

But before I took my daughter back home,
leaving this floating island, in tripling
thoughts of those who had forced me to leave

in the first place, in the uncoupling
of chains, esteemed a failure, I preferred it
that way. And never thinking I'd ever go back,

or that my voice would declare an end to exile
on my hidden planet, I fared forward
in banished light to the homeland I'd left

so long ago. I sailed headlong into my past—
as my daughter rushed into her future.

Piercing Notes

I'm on the point of finding a way to find
my way. After my daughter's recital,
with opening ears, I hear in piercing
notes, my own pierced cry that tells how a yellow
leaf collides with Indian Summer, surges,
and floats down. And tells how an iridescent
clock captures sounds in the deathless
flutter of non-stop ticking in the clockwork skull.

And how the clock's hands will fall one night
to cut off my head. To a primitive
brain—no psyche or science—it hums
the tune of the spheres, tuned to lost planets.
Headless, I find my heedless way, carrying my head
in my hands—carrying the held notes in my throat.

Exploding Flower

In a forensic analysis of Dylan's
exploding flower, I palm and hold his ear-
shattering poem.
Finger the word-bomb in both hands. Tongue it,
but that's no way to dismantle the triggering

device. Ignite the green fuse that blooms into boom-
force, where doom's theory drives me deep and deeper
into lyric destruction—
to love the words that appear to disappear
in their sounds. His fatal, silent stem bends

towards death. Words lisp and stream out with blood
from his mystic mouth. That mouth aches for a drop
of whiskey, no water.
Or screams for double-shots as the pen pierces his side.
More than a dram when the whole green-glass bottle is

out rowing with Caitlin in the morning.
On a drunken boat that hauls them away,
the Rimbaud of Cwmdonkin
Drive hoists his shroud sail, trailing 18 poems
in a dumbly dancing bay. But the fission

of his exploding flowers blasts my eardrums
and splits the atoms of my wounded words.

BLOOD STARS

Mud in his mouth, carnage of words, burden of love,
the easy beauty, as he said, *of death*—
It was easy to die with a list of dead words
in his shirt pocket. His suicide note:
a bullet hole in the forehead of the Soviet sky.
In a shower of slanting rain, through with words,
he passed by us. Standing on the platform,
he blamed himself for his life, and October,
1917. But Pasternak remembered
him *straddling a chair, like a motorcycle*,
flexed and free. Or in the railway
station, breathing in the coal dust and piston steam
of his deep voice, and hearing the solo
passages of his perfect escape, each word
a hammer blow, each fragment of his liturgy,
he chanted: *I leave my voice and name behind
as blood stars made by gunshot wounds in the brain.*

* Mayakovsky, the Russian poet,
   left a suicide note and shot himself.

Substitutions

The smallest keys unlock wonder in the guise
of the smallest words. The smallest things stand in
for larger ones. Hint at disappointment—
the substitution of one word for another,
one moment for the next in a lover's
quarrel with language. But the one-eyed translator
blinks and winks at criticism for faint praise.

The quiet life of heliotropes becomes
the odyssey of roses. Names and places
become thrill-seekers and fly off the page.
Substitute the way my mouth moves when I bury
it against your mouth—the smallest kisses
stand up and in for deeper ones as they substitute
and replace each other and claim their booby prize.

Capturing the Artist

My unpainted face never lets you down—
long hair, swept back off a low, beetled brow.
High broken cheekbones jut out like standing stones.
My jawbone is a carved ivory tusk.

Hollow eyes, set wide apart, and a Great Ape's nose—
mouth, a deep, red gash that slashes my jagged face.
In rioting zigzag, the discordant parts
gather the scattered bones for cave art's sake.

To capture the face is to possess it,
like one of Picasso's cubist works, or be
its victim. A Paleolithic cave painter

would render it on a cave wall with a spear
through the skull, a running man turning into
a wildebeest, or the other way around.

LOSERS WEEPERS

The hidden city is made up of hiding places—
If you live long enough, you'll find a place
where young girls drive off a pier and drown.
You'll hear a father's hidden wish for his
rebellious daughters: *May the devil shit
on their graves.* In the hidden city,
with its invisible courtrooms, only losers weep—

And if you live long enough, you'll come
to a hiding place in the hidden city
where those mourning the loss of their loved ones
die in a fire at a ceremony honoring the deceased.
But the thing of it is: we're all about to mourn,
if they don't mourn for us first. In the hidden city,
when it comes to happiness, finders keepers.

Only losers weep—And if you live long enough,
you'll hear from a deadhead sitting in
a hidden café behind his duck blind
that we all fail. *We all fail*, he says,
because we all die. Some of us die twice,
in our hiding places, happy that we've
heard it all before. Out walking the city
streets in our shrouds, like something out of Poe,
a last laugh flickers out even before
the devil has a chance to shit on
our graves. But buried away somewhere
in the hidden city, in their hiding places,
waiting out the virus that seeks out
all the hiding places, only losers weep.

Mapping the Hidden City

Drifting is a way of life—mapping
the city under your feet with holes
in the soles of your shoes. You almost
reach the point of letting go. Hunched over
open palms, you read the map of a broken
lifeline. A compass dial points north. Head tilted
back, it rotates south, searches for the route
that gets you what you need—winter coat
and Kodiak boots—more of everything
for your womb-to-tomb walk. Mapping eyes
beg everybody to leave you alone.
Alone but un-lonely, until you drift
away to map uncharted city streets,
psycho-geographer of our hidden city.

Street Busker

The street busker clings to his fiddle and bow.

His case is open for the dying fall of spare
change. Thin, bearded, he looks like a fisherman.
With the devil-in-his-music, he plays outside,

but not in Koerner Hall; only open spaces.
It's a straight-up choice to play in the street;
no interiors. No disclosing of his story—

the back-story of this scene. Busking,
he improvises the notes of it instead.
While the noise of posted signs shriek: *Occupy*

the City, he plays his rebel music
with ricochet bowing. On the fiddle's
frayed strings, he performs a far-out street song—

the hidden music of personal freedom.

Between My Toes

Wilderness eyes, shaded by a peaked cap—
hooded hawk's head, thin nose, mouth in shadow—
grey beard does the rest to hide the ghostly sway
of re-entering the city. Torn map on my lap

catches the sights. Thin ankles crossed—daddy long legs
lift out of ooze. Mud seeps between my toes.
Twisted sandals bind wet feet together.
Toenails weep blood. They're blessing bicycles

at Trinity-St. Paul's, but I don't
own a bike to bless. Everything was given
away to lightning thieves—years made and spent.
Left are good intentions and transmissions

of bad opinion—sweet mixture of highs and lows—
but nothing of the infinite jests of the past.

Begging at My Own Door

The beggared description of rain falling
in the alley is enough. Of all the hideouts,
this one is hidden on the slippery slope
of the begging years. With the prickling ache

in my twisted fingers, I secure the frayed
rope, just before I jump over the naked
puddles outside my own door to hide myself,
lift out of the mud and float above the trees,

a grey body hanging from a leafy bough.
Jump, jump, the hidden voices rise up from the past,
ghosting my cries, and the moment arrives

when all I have is all I ever owed.
And my debt is gratitude, a beggar begging
at my own door for something I don't own.

though
Cosmic Therapies

Therapy of the Final Approach

Arrive without traveling.
—George Harrison

My anatomized body flew from Earth
to Jupiter and back and felt sweat on the skin
all the way. Sky-watchers charted my time-
traveling trip in nanoseconds of wonder,
loss and healing. Against alien warnings,
I yearned for more time to seek out my sovereignty.
Then drifted, wandered and searched, went back
    and forth
in time and space. On any trip, I was out
orbiting the family planetarium.
Locked in my own machinery of words,
I quested from here to there—non-age to old age.
The final approach to the hidden planet
was perilous, not the launch and lift-off.
But why gaze at the stars when your navel will do?

Cosmic Therapy

Healing is an acquired taste, like driving
a stake through your own heart.
Doctors, dressed as lifeguards,
no longer guard the drained swimming pool.
I'm clearing out and don't need a receipt.
I'm through with staring at scars made
when I was young. I'm through with being
young. I've made a pact with the lake:
to shiver on the doomed shore before
plunging into dark waves. Despite surface
tension, I pull and push the past, then let
the quiet go. Up to the minute in my
cosmic therapy, I watch the nurses
and don't know how much to believe that once

I stood on Pier 21, suitcase at my side,
arriving, like my father before me.
But the time comes, in my hospital bed,
forced to remember my mother standing
in the kitchen giving an eloquent defense
of her first born. I was the accuser,
accused. I tried to shout her down
in a healing scream, but carried the weight
of it thereafter. On that aging Sunday,
I imagined I could find what I was looking for
away from home. Forced to go back to
the house with the *For Sale* sign swinging
on hinges—the debt I owe to the loss
I do not own is the therapy of defeat.

Therapy of the Last Ditch

Hunched, a hoop, in the therapy of the last ditch,
uprooted from the street, pushing a shopping cart
like a baby carriage, a hag in an ankle-length,
black leather coat, with a cigarette stuck

to her lower lip—is locked in the embrace
of her own pet theories about mental health—
Her black coat is too warm for July—
one of the thinly disguised therapies.

Still protective of her chaos, in the last ditch
effort, she remembers that yesterday
she was dancing in the kitchen—arms like wings

not drooping. Now her head is on the chopping
block, blade descending. But yesterday,
she was dancing in the kitchen.

Therapy of Faint Praise

I deserve it all, even as I blow
out the candles on the birthday cake,
or sing scat to the obscene caller.
I deserve it all: neighbor's killer dog, stagnant pool,
old jealousies, flat tires, traffic tickets,
smell of garbage on the breath, shit on the sole
of my shoe, knot-headed brother-in-law
and his bleeding nose. I deserve it all—
burrs I picked up on my walks through the woods
still clinging to my socks. If only the breath
would catch in the middle of a sentence
when you mention my name, if only you
could go back to 1964 more than
you already do, if only you could

make it about someone else, shouting
in the street, if only you could be free.
The faint praise I deserve when I'm shouting
in the parking lot that my muse is
a lousy girlfriend; shouting in the parking
lot that I kissed my daddy's ghost, zipped up
in his body bag; shouting in the parking
lot that it wasn't supposed to be like this,
shouting in the parking lot that I
deserve it all, and more, shouting in the parking
lot that spite is rust at the bottom
of your coffee cup, unable to stay
beautifully high in praise all those days,
but thinking about it even less than you do.

Therapy of Empty Rooms

> *My successes are not my own.*
> —Thomas Merton

He built her a house and furnished it with ruins.
What more could she want? He was caught up with
the way she moved through empty rooms. Taken in
by means of getting better, he left out the plans

he had for her in treatment. The therapy
began and ended with the collapse of the house
when they walked away. But don't look through his aging
words for traces of her body. Or examine

the way they stumbled and failed. He hid
the manuscripts and edited the personal
record. Then armed himself against plot twists,

especially betrayal. If you're looking for
him, ask the cosmic therapists. And if you're
looking for her, seek out the gossip of the stars.

Therapy of the Visible World

The whole earth is our hospital.
—T. S. Eliot, "East Coker"

The visible world is enough—like a long-tailed
hawk to the mountains, like the hummingbird's first flight
across your bay window. Instant daylight ascends,
hovers, dangles, shines—like sunlight on the highest
places, like eye-shattering waking in ever-
expanding eyes. The refraction changes
what I see, like a new day sending out
its frenzied invitation to see the world
in a new way. All that separates me
from the visible world is this appearance,
not budging an inch on the matter of dying,
and not giving up on living. To appear
to the world in a vanishing act perfected
from the beginning and to disappear on cue.

Therapy of the Trickster Sun

Looking up to see: two, long-tailed kites—
double helixes spiraling out of view.
Their spiky tails escape legends of gravity,
once observed in oriental annals,

or in a perfect sentence, such as:
Energy Equals Mass Times the Speed of Light Squared.
But the sun is up to its old tricks, telling
how it once appeared as a chariot and rider

that now lets darkness go along for the ride.
But healing comes for the first principle of the sun—
pinprick of light that ignites into absolute fire.

The long-tailed kites spiral back into sight,
tricking our eyes with healing sunlight.
A death spiral is also a therapeutic dance.

Therapy of a Mountain Session

Go up the mountain alone, not down.
Looking down makes you dizzy. Look up
in the spin of the eye—quicker than the sky.
Lone climber, cross the glacier to the word-

festival. See the summit from the valley
below. And go up the rock face to tread
on climbing words such as: *bouldering, crimp,*
and *first ascent*. But the base is where

you first set foot on the mountain. Start there:
calculate the angle from base to peak.
Learn what a mountain is—as it holds up its crest,

rising to the summit, yearn for the highest point.
And mark all vertices you traverse.
So with the Sherpa word for *freedom*, climb.

Therapy of Being in the World

Sent down from the aboriginal center

overlooking the valley, I snag and rend
winter's protecting veils that disappear
from this vantage point, like a shooting star.
At the rim of the abyss, my mind veers off

to the left. The wheeling of the earth tips
the balance of the riddle: ruins. My eyes
form axes with blind spokes of dead lights called stars.
I drop down on a dune. Daylight dismantles

death's invention—daylight once more, not daylight
still, in the signature of northern lights.
While I'm in the world, halted in my healing
by uncovering life's origin, I long

to go back, with the right of return.

Therapy of Living in a Terrarium

In the terrarium, green glass in black soil makes for an
  easy set-up.
All sadness is voluntary anyway.
It's the refusal to oblige anyone else, even the sun, gone in
  the head.
Or you can attend the socials.
With a new drink in your hand, you will be legislated back to
  mental health.
All the moments when what isn't supposed to, happens.
And they scrape you off the floor, or the walls.
A giant beetle lifts your hospital bed on its black back.
The bug walks away with it on all fours.
An earthworm picks it up and carries it the rest of the way
  through mud.
You step on a toad's jeweled back.
Your salamander's smile lifts the nurse's skirt.
Your weary climb is a lizard shedding its skin.
Its striptease is performed to the disquiet of angry applause.

Along your throat crawl two insects before and after
  the rain.
Red dust on your feet leaves rust stains on the doctor's shell.
The institution says your eggs are in one basket, like your
  lullabies.
For your sake, more worms in the terrarium are brought
  to a boil.
A croaking frog gently rocks on the sleeve of your lily pad.
"You mean something else," he says.
He is referring to the place.

The swamp music you play is ashamed of itself.
The ceiling you drift across simmers in the sun.
The window you skate on is a door.
The sanitarium comes to life with croaks, hisses and chirps.
And so do you.
Your mouth is a dark, seamless pocket filled with dirt.
And one of your therapies is life in a terrarium.

Therapy of Losing Your Mother Tongue

First to go, the mother tongue, no longer
speaking the way my mother made me.
Language was lost to the schoolyard babble
and the *f-word*. It was like wearing a false nose

while starting a grass fire in the flats,
or leaving teeth marks on the front porch. Foreign
words I didn't know then in 1955,
like the words *home* and *mother*. She sat by

the window, weeping. My chin barely cleared
the windowsill. I was looking out at the train
yard and could hear the thumping of shunting

trains and my mother's cry. It was like taking
something apart to see how it works: a watch,
a toy train, a radio, my mother's cry.

Therapy of Absence

There comes a time when you go back to wearing
a faded red paisley shirt. No longer
resisting failure, or the fate of the climate,
you plot a coup but can't get through enemy

lines. Instead, you discard black T-shirts.
Give away broken teacups and your daughters' dolls.
But box your books and keep the upright piano,

as if you know what they're for, bewildered
at sixty-one. A held note sticks in your throat,
but you can't hold it for long. So, Monday

is as good a day as any to wrap it up:
a question of deleting your rant from the rest
of the white noise to realize your absence
won't matter and shouldn't, but does.

Therapy of Being Hurt into Love

If you're starting with it, it hugs high walls,
hangs from balconies, binds archways, and wraps
itself around poles—rises up from sewers,

lets blood flow under the bridge, with dark laughter
to end where you started from—night. Night that
hurts you into love—what you recall

your mother's sunken eyes, black hair and thick eyebrows.
Hands fall between her knees, in quickening
applause, as your father returns from the seacoast

to cut the cord with moonlit scissors.
Her wounds of water and blood heal us all
in the therapy of being born and reborn.

Now, the way you turn her memory into love—
your hurt mouth leeching to her dark healing power.

Therapy of Losing You

Everything begins with a single gesture,
a look, especially a touch, and ends
that way, as if celebrating ruin
with love songs. Now, the mystery caller
whispers in your ear: *What's the mystery?*
Everything must go, even as you say
it won't last, it won't last very long.

Lost in being together: not moving
the compass needle when you're sixteen
or sixty-one. Lost in this waiting by
the collapsed bridge and railway trestle.
We've lost the schoolyard, the lake, the creek, and
    the woods—
and are lost now in the knowledge that *waiting*
is over—lost together and no longer young.

Therapy of High-Climbing

This morning, my high-climbing words aspire
to silent heights. Aware of fatal light,
ravens rise to meet them over mountain forests,
foothills, shrub-land and plains. Over Lodgepole Pine
and Douglas Fir, a lone falcon responds.
Now, my words unfold their wings and soar in
alpine light. Inside them, remote, lost with the sun

below the eye, high places change them. They climb up,
singing aboriginal hymns. No need
for the word *music* when everything's in sync.
High-flying words for high-talking birds—
but they wake to the beat of a sun hand-drum.
And squawk the sunrise's morning song.
Inscribed on the tongue or throat with no other way

of recalling it, their conversation
is an epiphany of beginnings.
Free to trip through cliffs and jags. When they find
themselves on the mountain, they live in
the bird's eye view. Along the sheer drop down,
a red-tailed hawk trails with sounds, high-climbing,
and my words aspire again to silent heights.

Therapy of Sorrow

My body lies down in an empty room, haunting
the house on Brunswick Avenue. I get used to
the white door, yellow curtains, falling clock
and dog's dish at the back door. Putting on shame,

I tuck away all judgments. Shelter myself
from how bits drain away. Nothing I can do
to gain what was asked for, calling to get my own back.
What about that tattooed woman squatting on

a blue crate outside the fruit stand with coins that trickle
down the gullet of her paper coffee cup?
My vanished coin is among the nickel-plated copper

and silver ones that funnel into her hands. Her thick
refusal is a hair's breadth of grief in my grasp,
sorrow's therapy when she won't give it back.

Therapy of Coming and Going

The one born to kill you is in the neighboring
town. Or maybe, next door. Or down the road,
kicking up dust with steel-toed boots. Or walking
on a frozen pond, or flying in tonight
on the first kiss. Or already sitting there,
waiting for you, asking: *Where have you been?*
The one dying to leave you is already
walking away. Or in the neighboring town.
Or maybe, next door. Or down the road, kicking
over traces with her boot heels. Or walking
on a frozen pond. Or flying away tonight
on a flying saucer. Or already sinking
her teeth into your goodbye, asking, *What
did you expect?* But the one I'm after

is already on the escalator
that carries her off. Little black dress,
dark skin and long legs—off they go.
Shift. Look up. Ride your eyes along the black
handrail—don't just sit there,
but you do, locked in the embrace of your own
pet theories about mental health.
And on your table in the food court:
two pairs of glasses, a book, *No Man
Is An Island,* a black jacket too warm
for July. You're protective of chaos,
in case someone stops you from coming
and going: one of your thinly disguised
attempts (as you come and go) of *cosmic therapy*.

Therapy of Silent Films

Tih Minh (1918), take me into your vast house,
Through the listening rooms,
With ornamental tables, carved staircases,
And portraits of limp women, sleeping.
Let me touch all the sobs of their breasts,
Like a beloved assassin,
Burdening anguish, moaning voluptuous hymns
To the polished skull on the table,
Shatters of stillness, inset with burning shells.
The pearls that drown their eyes
Drown us in waking horror,
With statues murmuring
The faint greed of paranoia.
Lift the skin of time

To find disquieting sleepers dreaming
They are children
With romantic afflictions
And the flowering shells of solitude
They wear, like hysterical bouquets.
Early, I was the skeleton (man or woman)
At the ivory feet of the voluptuous Theda Bara,
Whose anthropomorphic body
Was/is as corrupt as
The Isotta-Fraschini of the murmuring 20's.
Imagine her body, now dead,
As the automobile,

—continued

Delirium, or the stilled bird, descending
To pick clean my bones with tremors of doom.
I touch the jeweled asp adorning
Her breast, death and desire,
Beyond dark, or forbidden love.
I am talking about remorse,
The chimerical destroyer, desperately
In love with the man-eater.
I'll take my place among photos of Garbo
In *Wild Orchids* (1929), in the sleeping city.
Or in the immeasurable garden, I'll be like Garbo
And the beautiful Robert Taylor in *Camille*.
Or the World War I lovers: Cooper and Hayes—
As poisonous as the same glance that went between them.
Or the drowned eyes of child-women:
Lillian Gish, May McAvoy, Mary Pickford (1927)—

All the bee-sting lips and dreaming eyes, now silent.
Yet all these mirrors shatter, glamorous lipstick
On a cigarette or a glass. We come to it now,
Especially the lips of Hedy Lamarr.
And one thing is certain. Their angelicism,
Without genius or love, lurks and limps with death itself
In the presence of that desire. And silent,
They sink through boredom, sinking in shadows
Of Error and Fame. And they do not touch
My darkening soul fluttering like a moth
To the flaming of nightmares, or the despair of old films.

And do not touch me when I leave the house, dark
    and empty,
With wet ashes on my fingertips. When my body,
    too, is a spice
bowl, like Betty Grable's—a pomander of broken promises.

Therapy of the Echo

Words that dwell in me (ghosts or angels)

correspond in direct contact with the dead.
The sickness of knowing the higher order
of language; that silence is eloquence—

even as I defy the words; betray them.
They're too much for me and the unrehearsed
resolutions and unrecorded narratives

that reside in me, whispering: *The real horror
is losing a loved one.* The lost echoes,
after any massacre, heard at the beginning
but missed at the end when the conversation

is moved to the brink of the last silence—
I never hear the details of the echo—
the bones that plead to be heard as my ears bleed—

details that astonish another deaf night.

Therapy of Scavenging

Not that I failed, but erred, made mistakes
in my scavenging days—gains and losses.
Maybe, I was defeated as a way
of getting by. That in a place like this,
there's more to it than beauty or bloodshed—
Beyond diminishing returns
in the dumpster—the city's lost and found—

the place is littered with recycling
bins for raccoons and rats to feast on.
And what the scavenger hears when I'm here,
picking up treasure from the trash,
or unspooling the string to find my way back,
still frantic from the frenzy of the maze,
and unable to put the pieces together

again. Or pick over how things turned out
and discard them in the face of past hoarders,
still holding onto my glass, half full or half
empty in defiance of your overflowing
cup. And what's wasted and what's given away
no longer signify falling in the wheeling
of the seasons. But the way salvaged street-

light writes itself on my scavenging eyes.
I balance like an egg on a tagged wall,
always about to fall. Not erring
in the downward direction, never to be
let into the junkyard again, scavenger
of pluses and minuses, defeated,
if not less broken, no less victorious.

Therapy of Reading the Woods

Easy this time, unexpectedly, on retreat
north of Sharon, in a cycle of prayers
and simple meals, I traipse through deep shade
in the healing woods. Such remoteness is
an unstopped heart that seeks the terrain of why
I came here in the first place: to walk, read and grieve—
to pay the debt I owe to you in a place
like this—a debt to loved ones and deserted
friends—no *just cause* in the long view of lost time.
In the woods, a way to read the curative trees,
returning to the place that I remember
many Augusts ago—a picnic
with my mother and father, and the way
I grumble when we penetrate the woods.

In a flight pattern, crows straggle sunflowers
across the sky that bears them away.
A hummingbird swings from side-to-side,
up-and-down, against the intruders.
Blurred flight shatters the crystal waves of
rapid wing beats. It hovers in place
until it finds the flight pattern it has
longed for all its life, its sudden design.
I return now with the lost days that trail me
and carry books in a black rucksack, in case
prayers fail. A book lies in my open palms.
As part of my treatment, I read the woods.
The cure is sunlight on leaves, unexpectedly,
under a canopy of healing trees.

Therapy of Stargazing

Dreamed of in this lifetime, a new world,
brokered, just beyond *now*. As in
Gonzalo's dream, no social rank,
treason, or crime. And when the ark
of the planet is tempest-tossed,
gazing on stars for signs of intelligent
life, haven of opposites
in the execution of all things.
No traffic; no names. Unknown letters
of a new alphabet. No literature lost.
No personal losses; no riches;
no poverty; nothing bought or sold;
nothing owned, or exploited. No
oppression, or bonds. No danger

beyond plenty. No energy consumed.
No work—just idleness for all. All the time
in the world and all the room—in the simple
future, everyone will be fed from the same
disagreements and agreements.
Technology will assume its technique.
Weapons will be made into works of art.
Wishes will be granted before you jump.
Your breath will be sustained by a lullaby.
No more arguing with the dead. Intricate
questions will be answered with dewdrops
on ferns—and be just as true. No paradise.

—continued

No need of perfection. Tonight, when the whole
world is a hospital, and when the mystic
trumpeter blows us all sky high,
no need of cosmic therapy
on a starless night. No therapy
of the last ditch, of faint praise,
of empty rooms, of the visible world,
the trickster sun, a mountain session,
of pretending to be in the world,
of living in a terrarium,
of losing your mother tongue, of absence,
of being hurt into love, of losing
you, of high-climbing, of sorrow,
of coming and going, of silent films,
of the echo of words, of scavenging,
of reading the woods, of the cure of stargazing.

Epilogue

Until Every Sky Repairs Its Stars

Climbing over red terrain, across new
pathways, and crawling on my hands and knees
in red dust, I was home. Everybody

was talking about getting out. I was
stepping in with the blaze-bright lights of sun dogs.
Astonishing to watch, no longer a victim

of yesterday, today or tomorrow,
I stayed up half the night, despite the curfew,
and wondered what the last blink would bring—

what new *twinklings* it would hold—brighter than
I knew and know, mapping what I see and don't.
I charted each breath it took to move: to go

where every sky repairs its stars and every
ocean rides again with millions of blue whales.

About the Author

Anthony Labriola's work has appeared in such publications as *The Canadian Forum, PRISM international, Lo Straniero, Vallum: New International Poetics, Still Point Arts Quarterly,* and *Passion: Poetry.* He has had several collections of poetry published, including two others by Shanti Arts—*The Rigged Universe* (2nd ed., 2020) and *Birds and Arrows* (2017).

Labriola was born in Italy but grew up in Canada. He comes from a large family, and many of his siblings are artists. He is married to his childhood sweetheart, Louisa Josephine. They have five grown children—each an artist in his or her own right.

Labriola's love of poetry began at a young age when he first read Dylan Thomas's *The Force That Through the Green Fuse Drives the Flower.* The same force drove him to write with a focus on mystical realities. The theater also held a strange fascination for him, and he acted in, directed, and wrote many plays. After graduating high school in the late 1960s, he studied English and French at the University of Toronto, received a B.Ed. in English and dramatic arts from the Faculty of Education, and an M.A. from the Graduate Center for the Study of Drama. He taught English, drama, and performing arts for thirty-two years. He was also Curriculum Chair in the Arts and was inspired by the talents of his students.

Labriola now lives in Toronto, Ontario, Canada, and teaches Life Writing at Seneca College.

Shanti Arts

Nature ▪ Art ▪ Spirit

Please visit us online
to browse our entire book catalog,
including poetry collections and fiction,
books on travel, nature, healing, art,
photography, and more.

Also take a look at our highly
regarded art and literary journal,
Still Point Arts Quarterly, which
may be downloaded for free.

www.shantiarts.com

www.ingramcontent.com/pod-product-compliance
Lightning Source LLC
Chambersburg PA
CBHW022107040426
42451CB00007B/158